Hi, I Have A TBI

Michael Jarzenski

Dedication

This is for Traumatic Brain Injury Survivors. I am one of them. By looking at me, you couldn't even tell.

You can't see the side effects I live with.

You cant see the pains I suffer.

Without the scars, I probably look just like a normal chef.

Living with a TBI (Traumatic Brain Injury) is not only difficult but a different situation for every survivor. So to all those living with the pains. Living with the hard side effects that may have changed their life, this is for you.

This book is dedicated to the support I've had throughout these hard years. The strong people who continued to check in on me when I was struggling, and the ones who have helped me build Feel Good BBQ into the restaurant I've always dreamed of.

This dedication is for my family, my friends,

and the people I know I can call, and they would cancel all their plans to make sure I'm okay.

Even though I refuse to call, I know I have the option.

Those of you who hold that level of love, just know that you will always have a special place in my heart.

This dedication also goes to the wonderful team that helped put this all together, from the account manager to the editors and my sister, the photographer for the cover. Without all of you, it might have taken me six years to accomplish this.

Acknowledgment

This acknowledgment may read a little differently, but that's because this book is unique. I would like to express my gratitude to the individuals who played a pivotal role in shaping the stories within this book.

To those who took a chance on me in my career, I want to acknowledge your faith in me. You could have easily chosen another candidate, someone with more experience and a degree. Yet you saw something in the young kid—someone who lacked credentials but possessed a burning passion for their chosen path. To those who invested their time and gave me an opportunity, you will always hold a special place in my thoughts.

To the doctors who saved my life, I wish I could personally know each of you. I wish I could extend my hand in gratitude and thank you for granting me the chance to continue walking this earth. During the time of the accident, you were confronted with challenges beyond our imagination. It was the peak of the Covid pandemic, and hospitals were inundated with patients. Despite it all, the team that saved my life gave nothing less than their best, dedicating themselves wholeheartedly. From the surgery that commenced at 11 p.m. and lasted until nearly 6 a.m., you worked tirelessly throughout the night. You saved the life of a man to whom you had given a mere 7% chance of survival. I cannot emphasize enough the depth of my gratitude for the incredible work you performed.

CONTENTS

Page Blank Intentionally

Chapter 1

The Promise of Tomorrow

"I have realized that the past and the future are real illusions, that they exist in the present, which is what there is and all there is."

- Alan Watts

The concept of time is an interesting one.

We are bothered by the past while we live in the present, all while we keep pondering over what the future holds for us.

Is tomorrow promised?

Nobody knows.

We are so consumed with the promise of tomorrow that we forget to live in the present. We forget to cherish the moments in the present in hopes of reliving them in the future.

What is meant for the future certainly requires a little action and planning but obsessing over it while forgetting to live in the present is an idea that will leave you with nothing but misery in the end.

We live in a world where we like to think that we know that everything is going to be okay, but sometimes it doesn't work like that. Life, as we know it, has its ups and downs, and things just happen without any real explanation. It could be a normal day for you, just like it was for me.

You could be taking your motorcycle out for a ride just like you always do, but the next thing you know, you wake up in a hospital, where they tell you that you had been in an accident and had open-brain surgery. You remember the freedom of the wind blowing against you as you ride your motorcycle, but they tell you that you have twenty-seven staples in your skull along with a tube in your brain that drains the blood out of it. They tell you that they are not sure when you can leave the hospital, but you remember that before you closed your eyes, you were a free man riding against the wind, enjoying the sun as it shone.

Now, all you see is the hospital ceiling that looks like dark, gloomy clouds that have taken over your life. You were all ready for the plans you had for the future, the promises of tomorrow, but now you just lay in the hospital bed, unsure of when you will be allowed to leave.

However, unfortunately for this story, I don't remember much of my time in the hospital or at the time of the accident. My memory is fuzzy, even about the time I spent after the hospital; all I remember are just little blimps of all those events. That is my past – a past that I wish I could recall, but maybe my brain has just suppressed all those events, or I don't remember them because of what I went through.

I remember that I laid in the hospital bed, terrified of what was going to come. I had been told the damage of the injury was unclear. They weren't sure if the injuries would take months or years to heal. The uncertainty did not end there; there was the possibility of me never recovering from it throughout my lifetime.

Was I going to return home, or would my life be in a hospital? Nothing was answered at that time. If I were home, would I be able to do anything? Would I be able to return to being an Executive Chef? Unsure if I would live my life the way I wanted, I just prayed to be able to live the way I did before.

A normal life. That is all I wanted.

This unfortunate incident took place during the COVID-19 pandemic, and I was not allowed to see any of my loved ones. I was left to ponder what had happened to me and what *would* happen to me as I laid by myself, all alone in the hospital room with nothing but beeping machines as my companions. Most of my thoughts about the past, present, and future took birth at the point in my life where I was left alone to understand what happened and for what reason. It was supposed to be a day like any other, yet it was completely different.

I wrote my story seven hundred and twenty days after my accident. That incident made me think a lot about what tomorrow actually is. Tomorrow is sometimes the same as today, and tomorrow can sometimes be the same as yesterday.

I'm trying to say that it is uncertain what tomorrow is. It could be the best day of your life or the worst day of your life. Tomorrow isn't something that can be promised or guaranteed. The thought of living life without knowing what is going to happen next has always scared me. The uncertainty that life holds is something to be scared of. You could be living your best life one day and then be on the verge of death the next. After my accident, the uncertainty in my life has increased even more now that I live with a TBI, Traumatic Brain Injury.

With the damages that were done, some side effects still stuck with me after the accident. Every day goes by with little hope that I will someday live a normal life, free from those side effects.

How can I look at the future with a promise that life will be okay when even the doctors are not sure if the side effects will ever go away?

Is there a promise for tomorrow, or do we live today and accept what we have today?

But when you think of today, what is today?

Is today our last moment?

Does today have a resemblance to yesterday?

Will we see our mistakes of today so we can remember them tomorrow?

My point is that tomorrow might not come, so why not live each day like it is our last? Live life, make memories and do the things you want to do because, at the end of the day, tomorrow is not promised.

Regardless of what we have today, we find comfort in the idea that tomorrow will be better. Let's say you have some bills that are past due dates, but tomorrow you have a payday, so you know that payday will make things better. You find solace in something that is to happen tomorrow when tomorrow is not promised. Payday comes, but all of a sudden, your car has a problem with it, and it won't start. You sit in your car, filled with frustration, wondering how you will make it work. You decided to put it off and let a mechanic deal with it tomorrow, and then you can also take care of the bill tomorrow.

Now the problem comes when reality kicks in. The bill belonged to your phone company, and they decided to shut off your service today since it was already past the due date. The illusion of a perfect tomorrow broke for you, and you made today troublesome for yourself in hopes of finding a better tomorrow.

As Albert Einstein said, *"The distinction between the past, present, and future is only a stubbornly persistent illusion."*

What does stubbornly persistent illusion mean?

When we consider each of these words at their core, being stubborn means not changing one's attitude or position on something. Being persistent means continuing firmly in the course of action despite difficulty or opposition. An illusion is a thing that is likely to be wrongly perceived by one's senses.

So, now the question comes, what did Einstein really mean?

Allow me to explain.

In my opinion, looking at the past, present, and future with distinction is nonsense. The time that has passed by is a dead person in the grave, by example. No one has brought the dead back to life just by crying over it.

So, what is the past in that perception? Past is all those memories, those people, and those stages of life that you have been through. Enjoy all that has gone by but do not dwell in what has gone by, for you cannot bring back what has gone by, but you can live in the moment and appreciate all that lies in front of you.

People will try to explain the past and the future to you and try to bring fear of the unknown to you. *You could lose what you have; the path of life has been robbed of many people,* is what they might say. But it is always good to remember that the moment you live in lives on because of you.

Life moves on. The time that is to come, which is the future, is unpredictable. Why do we cling onto hopes of something that we are uncertain about? Life goes on without a care for what you hope for. The present is something we live in, yet we take it for granted. We often stay stuck to memories of our *yesterday*, which is not the right way to live our *today*.

Live today the way you want to, so you do not cling on to hopes of the future, and when in the future, you do not look back on the past, hoping you had done what you wanted to.

Tomorrow is not promised, and it never will be.

Make every single second count and live life like it is meant to be – without a care in the world!

Chapter 2

Brains, I Don't Recommend Them

"Everything we do, every thought we've ever had, is produced by the human brain. But exactly how it operates remains one of the biggest unsolved mysteries, and it seems the more we probe its secrets, the more surprises we find."

- Neil deGrasse Tyson

As someone who has suffered from a TBI, I can tell you firsthand that brains are not all they're cracked up to be.

While the human brain is often touted as the most complex and remarkable organ in the body, I can attest that having a damaged brain is far from a blessing.

While I personally don't recommend brains

based on my experience with a TBI, I do understand the paradox of this statement. Brains are indeed incredibly important, as they are responsible for our thoughts, emotions, and overall functioning. However, let us not forget how fragile our brains are at the same time. In the same way, one accident was all it took to give me a TBI. A TBI that no one can tell me if it'll get better or worse as my life goes on.

Despite this, it is important to understand that our brain is incredibly adaptable and resilient. With proper care and attention, it can recover from injury and continue to develop throughout its life.

As much as I can talk down on the brain, it's also the powerhouse for doing amazing things. Our brain is like a giant computer that controls everything we do. It's made up of tiny things called neurons; in my case, after my injury, those neurons don't fire the right way, and they don't work how they are supposed to.

But, what are neurons?

They are like tiny electrical wires that send messages to each other. Now, if I try to explain the brain and how it works, I will probably fail. It is such a complex thing that people that have been studying it for years have not been able to uncover all its secrets.

However, this is what I can tell you about the brain. We have neurons, and those neurons have a body and long arms called dendrites that reach out to other neurons. When a message is sent from one neuron to another, it travels from the end of one dendrite across a tiny gap called a synapse and into the dendrite of the next neuron. A synapse is like a tiny electrical switch that opens and closes to let the messages flow between neurons.

What do those messages do? The messages help us think, move, feel, and remember things.

There are many different types of neurons in the brain, and they all have different jobs. Some neurons are like messengers that send signals to the muscles, telling them when to move. Other neurons help us process information, store memories, and control our emotions. All of these processes happen incredibly quickly, in just a fraction of a second, to be exact.

It is amazing to think about all the tiny electrical signals and chemical messages constantly flying back and forth in our brains, helping us to do all sorts of things. And that's just the tip of the iceberg when it comes to how the brain works! There is still much left to learn and discover about the organ that is fragile yet so strong.

So, what damage did I suffer? If you asked my doctors, they would tell you that my brain hasn't been damaged physically, nor are there any signs of damage. My brain had been rattled around, that's for sure. I had severe concussions, and because of that, my neurons and synapses got reworked and reorganized to the point where they don't work the way they're supposed to. Some of them feel like they have been misplaced and just don't work at all.

I can wake up tomorrow, and my brain could be completely fine; I could wake up ten years from now, and it would be fine then; or the TBI could be something I would have to live with for the rest of my life. They can't give me a timeline for when I will heal because my doctors do not understand how my brain will heal from what it has suffered. There is still so much research and development that neuroscientists are doing on the brain to try and figure out how it works, heals, and all that it consists of.

I was a healthy person before any of this happened, but now I find myself struggling with chronic headaches. I deal with migraines regularly. I have a constant headache almost 24/7, followed by an occasional migraine. It has been three years since the accident, and I have not had a single day since the day of the accident that I didn't have to deal with a headache.

Dealing with a TBI is an exhausting process. Every day, I am reminded of the limitations my TBI has placed on me. I struggle with basic everyday tasks that once came easily to me, and I sometimes have trouble remembering things I used to know by heart.

My life right now is a constant reminder of what I used to be; it is a constant struggle to stay positive and motivated. My TBI has shown me the fragility of the brain and the devastating consequences that even minor disruptions to its function can have.

The one thing I can say I have learned from my experience regarding my brain after the TBI is that once you come to peace with death, you really begin to live peacefully.

Let's be honest here.

We all think about death; it is inevitable.

We think about what our final days will hold.

We need to know that once we are gone, we will be content with what we leave behind. The stress of wanting to be content with the legacy that we leave behind is slowly eating away at us. We let societal expectations shape our expectations of what constitutes a successful legacy.

This can lead to a narrow and distorted view of what truly matters and what will bring us lasting contentment.

Ultimately, it is important to recognize that our legacy is not just about what we leave behind but also about how we live our lives, the relationships we build, and the positive impact we make on those around us.

Despite my experience with a TBI and a fragile brain, I cannot help but be in awe of the brain's intricacies and how it shapes us as individuals. Every day, I am reminded of its strengths and limitations, yet it still fascinates me. The human brain is truly a mystery and has been given a unique insight into its complexities as a result of my TBI.

While I would not wish an experience like mine upon anyone, I am grateful for the lessons it has taught me about the delicate and enigmatic nature of the human brain.

Chapter 3

Chef TBI

"Cooking is like painting or writing a song. Just as there are only so many notes or colors, there are only so many flavors – it's how you combine them that sets you apart."

– Wolfgang Puck

For this part of our story, I want to go back to when I was growing up. Growing up, we didn't spend much time together. My parents worked multiple jobs, leaving little time for us four siblings to bond. My older sisters were always busy with extracurricular activities such as pageants, plays, cheerleading, and sports. We were always on the go, never really spending quality time together as a family.

However, Saturday nights were different. We would all gather at my great-grandma's trailer in the trailer park, and those were the only times I felt like we were truly happy as a family. It was a strange feeling because we were generally content, but something about being together in my great-grandma's cozy abode created a different atmosphere.

During those Saturday nights, we would forget about our outside problems and enjoy each other's company. I slowly began to realize that the reason for this was partly due to my great-grandma's cooking. Her food brought us together and filled us with warmth and comfort, creating memories I will always cherish.

My great-grandma's in-house cooking was a huge part of those happy Saturday nights with my family. The comfort and joy we felt from her delicious food made us forget about the outside world's problems. As a kid, I began to appreciate the power of a good meal and its ability to unite people.

I knew then that I wanted to share that feeling with others and bring comfort and forgetfulness to their lives through my cooking. There's something special about sitting down to a good meal with nothing else on your mind but enjoying the flavors and the company around you.

Certain meals can bring up good memories and create a connection that's hard to explain. That overwhelming comfort inspired me to pursue cooking beautifully, thanks to those Saturday nights at my great-grandma's trailer.

My love for cooking started at home, where I experimented with different recipes, from breakfast casseroles to breakfast lasagnas. It was my way of bringing comfort to my family and sharing my passion for food.

But I wanted to take my cooking skills to the next level, so I enrolled in a culinary arts program at a career technical center during high school. It was my first time in an industrial kitchen, and I was in awe of the possibilities that lay before me. Being in the kitchen felt comfortable, and I knew I had found my calling.

While I was still a part of the program, I landed my first job as a line cook at Shady Hollow Country Club. It was a big deal for a 16-year-old, and I was excited to take on the challenge. The job exposed me to high-volume production and banquets, and I learned so much about the industry quickly.

My first job as a Shady Hollow Country Club line cook was challenging and rewarding. I was only 16, but the executive chef gave me a chance to prove myself, and I seized the opportunity. From that moment on, I knew I wanted to make cooking my career. The kitchen had become my second home, and I couldn't wait to see where my passion would take me next.

The camaraderie and sense of family that develops among kitchen staff is something special. We work hard together, often under intense pressure, and a deep sense of trust and respect grows between us. Even the shouting and occasional burns can't detract from the feeling of being part of a team.

Despite the long hours and hard work, I was in my element. Cooking was no longer just a hobby but a career path I was passionate about pursuing. The joy I had always felt from cooking at home was now multiplied by the satisfaction of creating dishes for others to enjoy.

Those experiences further fueled my passion for cooking, and I decided to pursue formal culinary education. I attended the Culinary Institute of America in Hyde Park, New York, where I learned about the true beauty of food and the art of cooking. During the program, I ventured to Boston, Massachusetts, where I worked at Fenway Park for a summer externship program after my first year.

Working at Fenway Park was a whole new level of high-volume production cooking. I wasn't just working in a concession stand; I was cooking for the big-ticket buyers in the upper suites, serving up meals for hundreds of people daily.

Despite the pressure, I relished showcasing my skills and pushing myself to new heights. Living in the city and being part of an amazing sports team made the experience all the more thrilling.

After working at different places and gaining valuable experience in the culinary world, I found myself back at Shady Hollow Country Club, where I had my first job as a line cook when I was only 16. It was kind of a full-circle moment for me, but I didn't plan on staying there for too long.

However, fate had other plans. The executive chef position suddenly opened up, and I knew I was a great fit for the role. I had already spent a few years there before high school and had just returned from college with fresh knowledge and skills. So, I decided to go for it and approached the general manager about my interest in the position.

When I asked the general manager for the executive chef position at Shady Hollow, he agreed to put me on a two-month trial period. I was only 20 years old then, which was very young to be an executive chef, but I was determined to make it work. Even though I wasn't fully prepared for the job, I had the drive and energy to figure things out.

During the trial period, I spent countless hours improving myself and learning as much as possible. I would arrive at 8:00 AM and wouldn't leave until 10:00 PM or later. I was constantly asking questions and seeking out new ways to improve. While challenging, it was also a great learning experience that taught me much about leadership.

I was determined to figure things out and improve myself. Every day, there were new things to learn, and I put in long hours to ensure I was doing my best. It was a great learning experience and one that I truly valued. Having a staff under me was a new and exciting feeling, as I was responsible for directing and connecting with them.

It gave me a sense of achievement and a sense of responsibility to ensure that I knew what I was doing and that my team was growing and learning alongside me.

I believe in building a team with the same energy and drive as me, as it creates an environment where we can all push ourselves to improve. It's important to me that everyone I work with is learning and growing, not just me.

I wanted my team to feel engaged and excited about their work, not just go through the motions daily. This approach has served me well, and I'm grateful for all the people I've worked with who have shared my passion for improvement and success.

I was determined to ensure that anyone who worked under me was learning and growing. It wasn't just about me learning new things and finding new ways to run the business; it was about everyone on my team doing the same. I wanted my staff to leave work feeling like they learned something new that day and left the job in a better position than when they started.

What connected me to this work was seeing customers happy and satisfied with their meals, feeling comfortable, and enjoying their experience. I wanted my staff to feel the same sense of enthusiasm when they came to work each day. It was like I had been put on this earth to create an environment where people could learn, grow, and feel fulfilled in their work.

It was a strange feeling when I realized that, but it was also one of the most rewarding experiences I've ever had. It drove me to continue building teams that shared my same drive, energy, and enthusiasm. When you have that kind of energy around you, it's contagious and makes you want to keep pushing forward. I've always believed that having a team that's willing to grow and learn together is one of the keys to success in any business.

However, as life had called, I had to part ways with Shady Hollow. My life had taken a new turn that I had to tend to.

After leaving Shady Hollow, I took a job as the general manager of a butcher shop called Hometown Meat and Seafood Company. This was about six months before the accident. I decided to step back from being an executive chef and take on a slightly calmer role due to my recent marriage.

While at Shady Hollow, I worked long hours; there were even times when I worked 24 hours straight. One event in particular, Member-Guest, required me to feed 200 people for breakfast, lunch, and dinner for three consecutive days.

At Hartville Hometown Meat and Seafood Company, I found the pace to be more manageable. I wasn't working the long hours I was used to and had more time to focus on my personal life. Working at Hometown Meat and Seafood Company was a refreshing change as it was a Monday through Friday job, with hours from 7:00 AM to 5:00 or 6:00 PM. The job provided free time to experiment with food and refresh my menu development skills.

As a general manager, I was involved in all aspects of the butchery, including the butchering and preparation of different meats, seafood, and fish. I had the opportunity to try out new recipes and experiment with different ingredients, which was a nice change from my previous role. Although I was familiar with butchery, the job allowed me to learn and expand my knowledge.

But despite the change in pace, my passion for cooking food remained the same. In fact, having more free time allowed me to experiment and play around with different foods. I had the opportunity to try out new recipes and techniques with steaks, pork, chicken, fish, and seafood. I was constantly looking for ways to create something different, something that no one else was doing.

I discovered that my love for playing with food was still very much alive and well. I made it my motto that "it's my job to play with my food." I enjoyed the challenge of finding new ways to cook and have fun with it. As long as I was having fun with it, I knew I would never stop being a chef.

Looking back, I'm grateful for those Saturday nights at my great-grandma's trailer, where I first experienced the power of a good meal. Without that foundation, I might never have discovered my love for cooking and the joy it brings to both me and those around me.

Chapter 4
Learning Patience

"Learning patience takes a lot of patience!"

-Tim Hansel

The journey of learning patience is hard to come by. In this fast-paced world, we want to finish everything and anything as fast as possible. I had a relentless desire for speed. I always looked for ways to make things faster and more efficient.

Impatience has always been a defining trait of my personality. I've never been one to wait for the right moment or opportunity. In my mind, there's no time like the present; if something needs to happen, it should happen immediately.

This mindset was especially evident when I entered the general manager's office and declared I was the perfect fit for the job. Looking back, I cringe at how naïve and overconfident I must have sounded. The truth is, I wasn't remotely qualified for the position, and it took a full year of hard work and learning even to come close to meeting the job requirements.

Throughout that first year, I struggled with my impatience. I wanted to be the best at my job immediately, without realizing that success takes time and effort. But the general manager was patient with me. He saw something in me that I couldn't see in myself and took the time to guide me through learning the ropes.

I threw myself into the job, determined to absorb as much knowledge as possible. I learned about everything from the gas lines to the exhaust hood systems, eager to prove my worth and make up for my lack of experience.

Looking back, I realize that my impatience was a hindrance rather than a help. But through the general manager's patient guidance, I learned the value of taking things slow and putting in the work to achieve success.

Reflecting on my journey, I can see how

impatience has been a constant theme in my life. I've always wanted things to happen immediately without taking the time to consider the bigger picture.

This impatience was especially evident in my early days as a chef. I was so focused on learning everything I could about the job that I lost sight of what was right before me. I became obsessed with cutting down cooking times, trying to find ways to make recipes that took ten or twelve hours in just six or eight.

But as I progressed in my career, I began understanding the value of patience. I learned that success takes time and effort and that there are no shortcuts to achieving greatness. This lesson was reinforced when I embarked on home renovation projects, where I once again tried to rush through things.

Through it all, I've come to realize that impatience is not always a bad thing. It can be a powerful motivator, driving us to achieve more than we ever thought was possible. But we must also learn to balance this impatience with patience, to take the time to appreciate the journey rather than simply rushing toward the destination.

From an early age, I always wanted things to happen quickly. Whether working on my car or pursuing a goal, I tried everything to speed up the process. But as I've grown older, I've realized that some things can't be rushed.

At 27 years old, I'm still learning how to cultivate patience. I've discovered there are no shortcuts to learning this essential life skill. Things happen when they happen, and I've learned to accept that.

One experience that taught me the value of patience was my motorcycle accident which I never wanted to happen. I have a TBI because of it; however, looking back, I can see that it was a turning point in my life. During the year-long recovery process, I had ample time to reflect on my life and focus on my mental health. Through this process, I realized that I wanted to become an advocate for others who struggle with similar challenges.

Today, I'm grateful for the accident because it has put me in a position to help others in need. As a mental health advocate, I use my experiences to connect with others who are going through similar struggles. Looking back, I can see that the accident was a pivotal moment that ultimately led me to where I am as an advocate for mental health.

Sometimes, the best way to learn is by taking a step back and reassessing everything. That's what I did during my recovery period after the accident. I took the time to reflect on my life, goals, and what truly mattered to me. I learned that rushing things only leads to setbacks and disappointment.

It was a hard lesson to learn, but I'm grateful for it because it taught me the importance of patience. When I tried to rush my recovery and return to work, it only resulted in me being back in recovery again. From that experience, I realized I needed to slow down and allow my body to heal at its own pace.

Nowadays, I apply the same principles to everything I do, including house remodeling and cooking. I've learned that taking the time to do things right is more important than rushing through them. Whether it's a ten-hour cooking process or a two-month remodeling project, I've learned to be patient and take my time to ensure that the result is something I'm truly happy with.

To this day, it is a learning process for me, and I believe it is something I will continue to learn throughout my life. I will spend my life figuring out what items need patience and what items don't. I guess the best way to phrase it all would be that it is a continuous learning process in which I hope to learn and grow as life progresses.

But the most important thing I've learned is that it usually doesn't turn out well when I rush things. Whether it's a car repair, a home remodel, or even cooking a meal, taking the time to do it right is essential. I've had plenty of experiences where I've tried to rush things and had a subpar result.

On the other hand, there have been times when I've taken my time and patience, and the result has been far better than I could have imagined. It's a lesson I continue to remind myself of every day.

My experiences with my motorcycle accident and recovery have also taught me the value of patience. It was a tough time in my life, but taking that year to focus on myself and my mental health was crucial.

Ultimately, I learned that patience is not just about waiting for things to happen. It's about being present in the moment, taking the time to do things right, and realizing that sometimes, the best things in life are worth waiting for.

As I reflect on my life, many moments have shaped me into the person I am today. One of the most impactful lessons I have learned is the importance of patience.

This lesson was ingrained in me through various experiences, including my recovery from a traumatic accident and my career as an executive chef. During my recovery after the accident, I was forced to learn patience. My marriage had become rough after the accident. About eight months into recovery, my wife and I decided to call it quits, leaving me alone. It wasn't an easy phase; I had to navigate it all by myself. Whether it was figuring out how to deal with my migraines or whether it was attempting to return to work, I had to be patient and learn it all and do it all for myself.

Similarly, in my career as a chef, I had to learn patience in the art of baking and dessert-making. Initially, I hated the precision and time it took to create these dishes. However, as I learned to follow the process and take my time, I realized that rushing the process only led to mistakes and imperfect outcomes.

These experiences taught me patience is key to achieving success and creating something great. It's not always easy, but taking the time to do things right and letting things happen naturally can lead to amazing results. This lesson has stuck with me and continues to guide me in all aspects of my life.

Chapter 5

July 12, 2020

My memory recalling the day it all happened is hazy; I don't remember much of the details of what happened after the accident, but this is the story of that eventful day as I remember it.

It was a beautiful summer day on July 12th, 2020, and I was feeling adventurous. My wife and I hopped on our motorcycle and took a ride to her workplace at the brewery. We strapped on our helmets, feeling the wind brush against our skin as we cruised down the open road. It was just like any other Sunday, but little did I know that this day would change the course of my life forever.

After dropping off my wife at work, I headed back home and spent the day with our dogs. I did some cleaning and housework, but as I said, my memory of the day was hazy. However, I distinctly remember feeling a sudden urge to get gas for the motorcycle before picking up my wife later that night.

It was a decision that would alter the course of my life.

Without thinking, I made the impulsive choice of not wearing my helmet, which was uncharacteristic of me. I hopped on my motorcycle, feeling free and alive as I rode to the gas station.

That day was the only time I ever decided to go without a helmet, and to this day, I'm not sure why I did it. Looking back, perhaps I thought it would be okay because the gas station was less than five minutes away. It felt as if it was just destined; I made all the mistakes that I normally never did. When I went out, I even left our dogs unattended.

Our dogs were well-behaved, and we usually chained them up just in case. On that day, I wanted to give them some time outside in the middle of July. In my mind, it was just like any other day, so I left the dogs outside while I went to get gas, assuming I'd be right back.

Unfortunately, my assumptions were wrong, and the day ended with a motorcycle accident that left me with life-altering injuries. The accident occurred about a quarter of a mile down the street from my house, in a small intersection right in front of someone's home. Witnesses reported hearing a distinctive crashing noise, and when they came outside, they saw me and the motorcycle on the ground while a vehicle was pulling away. Details about the vehicle were unclear, with reports ranging from a van to a car.

Thankfully, the witnesses called 911, and an officer arrived at the scene. However, due to my severe skull fracture and bleeding on the right side of my brain, I couldn't hold a conversation, leading the officer to assume I was drunk, high, and speeding. I was written off as being at fault.

Looking back, it isn't easy to piece together the events of that day, especially with information coming from various sources.

The people in the house where the accident

occurred said that it was not my fault, but knowing me and my nature, I could see myself trying to take responsibility for the accident to prevent any further damage. Unfortunately, that's just the type of person I am. From there, I was taken to the hospital, where I was treated for my injuries.

It was around 9:15-9:30 PM, and I was supposed to pick up my wife from work. Anyone who knows me knows that I'm very punctual, often arriving early and texting my wife to let her know. However, on that night, I didn't text her, causing her to become concerned. As the night went on, she tried calling and texting me with no response.

Eventually, a nurse at the hospital answered her call and informed her of my accident. My wife's friend drove her to the hospital, and my wife made phone calls to our families to inform them of the situation. It was fortunate that my family was in Ohio at the time, as they were celebrating my nephew's birthday. They were all able to come to the hospital to support me.

However, it was July 2020, the peak of the

COVID-19 pandemic. People were not allowed to be around each other, hospitals were overwhelmed, and it was a challenging time. My family arrived at the hospital around 10:30-11:00 PM, trying to figure out what was happening and the next steps.

My family was informed they couldn't see me due to the hospital's COVID-19 protocols. This caused them to panic, as they wanted to check on me and see how I was doing. The hospital staff couldn't give them many updates as they were still assessing my condition. They eventually informed my family that I needed surgery and that my chances of survival were only 7%.

They advised my family to say their goodbyes from a distance because they couldn't see me. This was a difficult situation to be in, and I couldn't imagine what my family must have gone through. However, I was fortunate enough to survive the surgery and come out victorious.

So after my family was told that they couldn't see me and that I had a slim chance of survival, I underwent surgery. The doctors had to prepare me for surgery as I had lost a lot of blood, and my skull was badly fractured.

After a successful six-hour brain surgery, the doctors informed my family about the extent of my injuries. They weren't sure if I would ever be able to see or hear again. They also thought I might have difficulty walking and speaking due to brain damage. There was a lot of uncertainty, and they didn't even know if I would wake up from the coma.

However, I was lucky enough to survive the surgery, and when I woke up much later after my family had been informed, I asked to go home. It was a surprising moment for my family, considering the extent of my injuries. The doctors had warned my family that I might not even wake up from the coma for weeks, months, or even years, but there I was, asking to leave the hospital just a few days later.

Although I was asking to leave the hospital, I was still unable to move, see, or hear with ease. I had a lot of difficulties in doing so. The damage that was done to my right eye and left ear made it difficult for me to see and hear. The doctors were unsure if I would ever regain my ability to see and hear properly. Additionally, I had brain damage that affected my speech, and the doctors were unsure if I would be able to walk again.

Despite these challenges, I was determined to recover and get back to my normal life. My family and friends were there to support me through this tough time, and I am grateful for their love and care. It was a long road to recovery, but with the help of my doctors, family, and friends, I was able to overcome my injuries and regain my abilities after I took about a year to recover.

After the surgery, I spent a week in the hospital recovering from my injuries. It was a slow and painful process, but I was determined to get better. I had to relearn basic things like walking, talking, and eating. Most of what I did, didn't have to be entirely relearned, with some of the things I just required a little assistance. It was a humbling experience, but it also gave me a newfound appreciation for life.

During my recovery, I had a lot of time to reflect on what had happened. I realized that I had made a huge mistake by not wearing a helmet. It was a decision that could have cost me my life. I also felt guilty about leaving my dogs outside without telling my wife. It was a careless mistake that could have had tragic consequences.

I had left our dogs outside without a mention of them to my wife. Somehow, they had escaped because neither my wife nor I had returned home after a long time because of my accident. This led to our dogs being caught by animal control, and it would just be an ordeal for us to deal with the matter. Luckily, my best friend and his wife went to animal control for us and decided to house my dogs while I recovered.

Looking back on my accident, I can see that it was a turning point in my life. It was a wake-up call that made me realize what's truly important in life. It taught me to appreciate the people I love, to live each day to the fullest, and to never give up, no matter how difficult the road may be.

I am grateful for the opportunity to share my story and hope it can serve as a cautionary tale for others who may be tempted to take unnecessary risks, especially regarding their safety.

Chapter 6
Embracing Solitude and Dissociation

"The soul that sees beauty may sometimes walk alone."
— **Johann Wolfgang von Goethe.**

Waking up in a hospital bed, uncertain of what transpired, was one of the most harrowing experiences I've ever faced. The subsequent journey through the hospital, my recovery, and the disintegration of my marriage plunged me into a profound sense of loneliness.

What does it feel like to be truly alone?

A once-vibrant sky bleeds into a colorless void

While silver and gold lose their lustrous charm

The wind's tender touch, now devoid of emotion

Fails to distinguish the warmth from the cold

Sleep becomes a fruitless endeavor, void of reprieve

As music's sweet embrace recedes to a distant murmur

The zest of food and sustenance withers away

And the company of others loses all its resonance

When loneliness consumes you, dissociation follows. You no longer crave the company or conversation of others, as it seems to lack purpose or value. Even after interacting, a hollow emptiness lingers.

A dark, unfathomable chasm.

This abyss appears to have no boundaries, no means to quell the relentless feelings of isolation. The darkness within seems inseparable from the flicker of light that seeks to guide you.

Thus, you retreat.

You hide yourself away, hoping not to impose on others or make them feel obligated to care for you. You withdraw, believing it shields those around you from the boundless void you bear.

You forge forward, solitary.

Adrift at sea, uncertain of the path to follow, you find yourself unable to discern the safest course. Yet, oddly, you don't care. Content to float amid the churning waves, you embrace the relentless swells that rock your vessel. Powerless to halt their advance, you accept their presence and cling to your life vest. Not quite wearing it, but holding on—just in case you're thrown overboard.

A storm looms on the horizon, heralding more imposing waves and fierce winds. Do you alter your course, or do you simply face the tempest head-on and see what fate befalls you? After all, it's just a storm. It can't be that bad. You're alone, so it threatens no one but yourself. And if the ship capsizes, what's the problem?

When loneliness engulfs you, there seems to be

no problem. It's an experience that can occur subtly, creeping in until it overwhelms you. As dissociation takes hold and the void expands, you become more detached from the world around you.

Loneliness breeds dissociation, prompting you to cancel plans with others, convinced that your absence is the key to their happiness. Yet the essence of your spirit remains, waiting for the storm to pass and the waves to subside.

What triggers loneliness? Is it the loss of a cherished loved one, be it a pet or a close relative? Does it stem from traumatic experiences, an inability to forge new connections, or perhaps a struggle to communicate our deepest feelings? Loneliness can arise from a myriad of sources.

It is said that there are three distinct types of loneliness:

- Intimate/Emotional
- Relational/Social
- Collective

Intimate/Emotional loneliness pertains to our bonds with significant others—those rare connections with whom we share our innermost selves, who understand our true essence.

Relational/Social loneliness reflects our yearning for quality friendships. Despite the semblance of connection offered by social media, we still crave genuine, face-to-face companionship.

Collective loneliness represents our desire for a supportive network or group that aligns with our beliefs, values, and aspirations—a community fostering a shared purpose and identity.

Loneliness, in all its forms, is an intricate tapestry woven from the threads of our human experience, a complex and delicate interplay of emotions that shapes our existence.

Is it possible to experience one form of loneliness without the others?

You might have a robust circle of friends who provide collective support yet still lack the profound connection needed to discuss your innermost struggles. Conversely, you might possess a deep emotional bond with someone, only to find yourself unable to connect with a close-knit group that genuinely supports you.

At times, you may feel adrift in all three realms of loneliness. You could find yourself emotionally detached from a partner or life itself, discover that your friends aren't truly present when you need them, or realize that you lack a network to share ideas and dreams with.

Life is a delicate balance of these three aspects of connection. There may be moments when one facet is absent, forcing you to lean on the others to compensate. This can prove challenging, as these connections can also be disproportionate—a strong intimate relationship might overshadow a fragile friend group, for example.

Finding our way through loneliness and connection is a lifelong journey as we try to keep a delicate balance between our emotional, social, and shared needs.

At the end of the day, my struggle lies in finding balance. I can lean heavily on my circle of friends when I need support, but unresolved internal issues still gnaw at me. As much as I long to set them free, I grapple with how to do so. When I attempt to share my inner turmoil, I'm haunted by the fear of burdening the listener.

Even now, as you read these pages, I wonder if I've invested enough time and effort to make this worthwhile to ensure I'm not squandering your precious moments.

I find it difficult to conclude this chapter, perhaps because loneliness is such a unique experience for each of us. To this day, I continue to search for the elusive inner peace I crave.

I wish I could offer answers on how to cope with these struggles, but I can't. These are insights that elude even me.

What I can say is that you are not alone. As I write this, I hope my words bring you solace, knowing that others share your battles. Our circumstances may differ, but our emotions can resonate.

You might have read this and recognized your own loneliness or the urge to dissociate. But in the end, I hope you realize that you are not alone. My journey through this unpredictable life has taught me that even when I feel like withdrawing from others, having people to turn to can be my saving grace.

Chapter 7

Insatiable Life

"The meaning of life is just to be alive. It is so plain and so obvious and so simple. And yet, everybody rushes around in a great panic as if it were necessary to achieve something beyond themselves."

-Alan Watts

In this world, we find ourselves submerged in a sea of faces, effortlessly catching glimpses of other lives. Our constant companions, the smartphones we clutch, grant us access to the curated realities of others in mere seconds. A swipe and a tap, and we find ourselves face-to-face with the lives we yearn for, even as we deny the comparison.

These visions, these moments we covet, linger in the recesses of our minds, coloring our mundane routines. As we do our work attire, we envision sun-kissed sands and sigh, dreading the hours ahead.

Ensnared in this cycle, satisfaction slips through our fingers like the very sands we long to touch.

So, how do we strike the right balance between pursuing our desires and fulfilling our obligations? Perhaps such a balance doesn't exist. Since the accident, I've grappled with an insatiable hunger for more. I strive to move my life forward, but satisfaction eludes me no matter what I achieve. I try to find joy in small pleasures, like creating cooking videos or exploring new parks with my dog.

I also attempt grander endeavors, such as remodeling projects, writing a book, or developing innovative culinary creations. Yet, even when I accomplish these goals, I find myself trapped in an unending cycle of dissatisfaction, effort, and eventual disappointment.

In my quest to understand this insatiable feeling, I've explored what it means and whether it can be changed for the better. But what does "better" truly entail? Life may not be about constant happiness, as good times come and go. The key might lie in recognizing and appreciating the good moments for what they are.

But is this awareness enough to bring us happiness? Can we simply accept that life will have its ups and downs and occasionally shatter us only to help us pick up the pieces? Where do we draw the line between seeking contentment and pushing ourselves to the breaking point?

As we ponder these questions, we may realize that our happiness and contentment lie in a delicate balance between ambition and satisfaction. Perhaps contentment stifles ambition, or our lingering dissatisfaction stems from an inability to discern what we truly want. The answers may not be easy to find, but acknowledging and exploring these questions can offer valuable insights into our pursuit of balance and happiness.

With this understanding, we can recognize that achieving complete happiness and satisfaction in life can feel like an elusive goal. Despite our accomplishments and successes, there's often a lingering urge to strive for more, to improve in various aspects of our lives. This internal struggle can be particularly challenging when things are going better than anticipated, yet we still yearn for more.

The question arises: are we genuinely content with our achievements, or do we feel we've fallen short in some areas? This sentiment resonates in many aspects of our lives, from culinary creations to the execution of cooking videos. We're left wondering if we could have done better if we truly achieved our best or if we settled for second place.

Ultimately, the critical inquiry boils down to whether we have high standards or expectations.

Understanding the difference between the two is essential. Standards serve as our baseline for quality, guiding our actions and decisions. They are the objective yardstick against which we measure our performance. On the other hand, expectations are subjective beliefs about future outcomes, reflecting our hopes and desires.

One is grounded in reality, the other in

imagination. One is based on fact, the other on belief. One represents what we need, the other what we want.

Discerning between the two can be challenging, especially when external expectations influence our internal standards. However, maintaining a robust set of standards can also elevate our expectations, driving us to strive for excellence.

As we progress on this journey called life, we often find that our experiences and circumstances shape the way we approach our standards and expectations. In our pursuit of happiness, recognizing and balancing these competing forces within ourselves can provide valuable insight into our motivations and desires, helping us navigate the path toward true contentment.

Standards and expectations influence every facet of our lives – from work and home to relationships and friendships. As we navigate the ever-changing tides of life, we must determine whether to adjust our standards or expectations to find balance. Are one or both held too high, leaving us in a perpetual state of dissatisfaction? Or perhaps both are set too low, trapping us in mediocrity?

Insatiability – the unquenchable thirst for something more – can be powerful. I first encountered this concept when discussing the pursuit of seemingly unreachable goals. After much introspection, I've realized that my sense of fulfillment doesn't stem from achieving personal milestones but rather from enriching the lives of others. Whether bringing joy through food or helping others realize their dreams, I find happiness in lifting others.

However, this selflessness doesn't always equate to complete satisfaction. For instance, when a customer praised one of my dishes as one of the best meals they'd ever had, I felt gratified but couldn't shake the feeling that I could have done better. It wasn't enough.

Why do I rely on others' happiness to validate my own? Why can't I find contentment in my achievements? Perhaps I'm still searching for the right goals, or my lofty expectations and even higher standards have trapped me in a cycle of perpetual dissatisfaction.

It may be time to reassess and recalibrate the balance between standards and expectations. Life is an ever-shifting journey, and finding comfort within ourselves might involve continual adjustments to this delicate equilibrium. Striking the right balance means maintaining our integrity without compromising our happiness, allowing us to escape the clutches of insatiability. Finding the harmony we seek might take time, patience, and perhaps even the occasional nap or cocktail.

Chapter 8
Anger Management

"Holding on to anger is like grasping a hot coal with the intent of throwing it at someone else; you are the one who gets burned."

- Buddha

This chapter is a testament to honesty, not only for myself but also for you, the reader. Let's face it, we all experience anger. We all have those moments we wish we could take back, knowing full well that our reactions were less than ideal. Anger is an inevitable part of life, and we each deal with it uniquely. Some of us turn to the gym to vent out frustrations, while others seek solace in food as a means of stress relief. A long drive with windows down and music blaring can do wonders for some. Yet, some unleash their anger on others, and some suppress it, letting it eat away at them from within. Whichever category you fall into, remember that you are not alone.

I had always buried my anger deep inside for most of my life. I would find ways to keep it contained, ensuring it didn't inconvenience or bother anyone else. Over the years, the gym provided some relief, but my true sanctuary was the kitchen. I found inner peace through cooking, immersing myself in creating new dishes. To some, this might sound odd, but to me, it was a form of escape. As I experimented with recipes, honing and perfecting them, my sole focus was on the food. The anger that had been simmering beneath the surface would dissipate, if only for a little while. However, things have changed since my traumatic brain injury (TBI). As much as I would like to suppress my anger, it refuses to stay buried. It resurfaces, demanding to be released, not in a violent manner, but more as a self-inflicted emotional backlash. In the most trivial of situations, my anger seems to have multiplied.

As an Executive Chef, it's my **JOB** to thrive in a high-pressure environment that many would consider "angry." I have to tackle situations that others might find overwhelming or chaotic. Oddly enough, in those circumstances, I manage just fine. I can juggle a frenetic Friday night on the line, multitasking as an Expo and Food Runner while fielding countless questions from staff about issues that don't really require my input. Before and after the accident, I held my own without any problems. But, the times I struggle most are when I'm alone. Why is solitude the issue? We often crave it, as it allows us to clear our minds and enjoy a little peace. But for me, that peace gives way to my inner demons.

These demons are manifestations of my self-criticism. I hold myself to impossibly high standards, expecting to excel at everything I do. For some inexplicable reason, I've always been my own worst critic. If I make a mistake, I berate myself, blaming and punishing myself for the error, even if it was completely beyond my control. This self-flagellation extends to cooking; if a dish doesn't turn out right, I assume I must have measured something incorrectly or mixed it improperly, or perhaps I was just impatient and rushed the process. I scrutinize every aspect of my life, getting angry when I skip a workout or overeat. If I botch a recipe, I take it as a personal failure. Instead of pointing fingers at others, I find ways to blame myself, taking on responsibility for any and every perceived failure.

On a personal note, anger is a normal emotion we all experience, but managing it can be particularly challenging for those dealing with a traumatic brain injury. Anger can be difficult to control when one has trouble focusing or regulating emotions after an injury. Often, trauma-related anger stems from feelings of powerlessness or frustration due to communication issues, social limitations, and other factors. Managing anger in these situations requires understanding the underlying causes and triggers while creating coping strategies tailored to each individual's unique personality.

However, just like any other challenge, it is possible to manage anger related to trauma when approached constructively, with patience and understanding. Here are some tips for coping with anger following a TBI:

1. Recognize the triggers: Identifying situations, people, or environments that tend to ignite your anger is the first step in managing it. Pay close attention to patterns in your behavior and emotions, and consciously try to understand what sparks your anger. Once you know your triggers, you can develop strategies to avoid or mitigate them, such as creating healthy boundaries, planning, or practicing positive self-talk.

2. Practice relaxation techniques: Mastering relaxation techniques is essential to managing anger. Deep breathing exercises, mindfulness meditation, or progressive muscle relaxation can help you calm down and regain control when you feel anger starting to build. Set aside time every day to practice these techniques so they become second nature when you need them most.

3. Seek support: Don't hesitate to reach out to

friends, family, or a support group to share your feelings and experiences. Opening up about your anger can be incredibly therapeutic, and those who care about you can offer understanding, encouragement, and advice. Building a strong support network is vital for emotional resilience and anger management.

4. Communicate assertively: Learning to express your thoughts and feelings assertively, rather than aggressively, is key to reducing frustration and preventing misunderstandings. Assertive communication involves being open and honest about your feelings while also respecting the feelings of others. Practice active listening, using "I" statements, and maintaining calm when discussing your emotions to foster healthy communication.

5. Maintain a healthy lifestyle: A well-rounded lifestyle is the foundation for overall emotional well-being and effective anger management. Regular exercise releases endorphins and helps

channel negative energy, while adequate sleep ensures you're better equipped to handle stress. A balanced diet, rich in nutrients, also contributes to emotional stability. Prioritizing these aspects of your life will make it easier to manage your anger.

6. Consider professional help: If your anger is causing significant distress or interfering with your daily life, don't hesitate to seek help from a mental health professional specializing in TBI and anger management. A qualified therapist or counselor can help you develop personalized coping strategies, address underlying issues, and provide guidance on your journey to better emotional health.

It is important to remember that the road to recovery is not the same for everyone, and my journey might resonate with some while others may find their own path. I hope that my experiences can provide some insight into what this journey could look like.

I recall the time when I struggled to identify the

triggers for my anger. It was a painful realization that I was the trigger. I was not happy with my own actions and my own self. Self-reflection was the key, and it took some time to acknowledge this fact. We often tend to externalize the problem, but sometimes, we need to look inward to find the root cause.

For a long time, I resisted the idea of relaxation. It seemed counterintuitive to rest when there was so much to fix. However, I've learned that self-care is not a luxury but a crucial part of the healing process. Relaxing and taking time for yourself can have a transformative effect on multiple aspects of your life.

Over the years, I came to understand that my support network was larger than I had ever imagined. Yet there was a fear—a hesitation to reach out to them. I was afraid to burden them with my struggles. But once I opened up, I realized that discussing these issues was not a problem; rather, it was a solution. It was a way of processing what was happening and finding a way forward.

Communication has been a cornerstone of my

recovery. Learning to be upfront about my feelings, not just with others but also with myself, was key to progress. There is a certain relief in expressing what you feel, in knowing that your feelings are valid and deserve to be acknowledged.

Maintaining a healthy lifestyle, especially when it comes to food, has had a profound impact on my journey. It's easy to succumb to the comfort of heavy, fatty foods or to rely on endless snacks as a coping mechanism. But I learned the hard way that these are just temporary fixes. Prioritizing healthier foods has led to a noticeable improvement in my overall well-being. A better diet truly does lead to a better life.

Finally, seeking professional help was a hurdle. I initially struggled to overcome the trauma. I was stubborn, believing I could manage everything on my own. I was hesitant to burden others with my issues. But accepting help turned out to be one of the best decisions I ever made. The guidance I received from mental health professionals was invaluable in navigating the complex emotions and challenges associated with TBI.

Every journey is unique, and while my experiences may not mirror yours exactly, I hope they offer some comfort and guidance. I want you to know that it's okay to struggle, it's okay to ask for help, and it's okay to take care of yourself. These are not signs of weakness; rather, they are steps toward healing and managing anger effectively.

Chapter 9
The Dark Days

"You may not control all the events that happen to you, but you can decide not to be reduced by them."

- Maya Angelou

Warning: Sensitive Content Ahead

To my dear mother, I advise that you **DO NOT** go through this chapter. Truly, I suggest that anyone with a tender heart or an aversion to painful realities do the same.

Middle school - I want to take you back to that tumultuous time when everything was in a constant state of flux. When our bodies, our minds, and our friendships were all morphing and changing at an alarming rate. The place where I found solace was an unlikely one - the TV show 'Ned's Declassified School Survival Guide.' I wasn't merely a casual viewer; I was a devoted fan, watching each episode with rapt attention as if it were a sacred text. It was a fun, quirky show that served as a guiding light, offering invaluable nuggets of wisdom on how to navigate the chaotic labyrinth that was adolescence.

The magic of the show lay in its relatability. From the school bully to the daunting math homework, every episode tackled a familiar hurdle. But then adulthood struck, and I found myself floundering. The training wheels were off, and there wasn't a guide in sight. Adulting wasn't merely about paying bills and attending meetings; it was a complete overhaul of life as I knew it, a journey fraught with uncertainty and high stakes.

Life, as they say, isn't easy. It isn't a leisurely walk in the park but a trek through a dense forest filled with twists and turns. At times, it throws curveballs at you, and sometimes it doesn't stop at just one. It's a relentless pitcher, hurling one after another, each one faster and more unexpected than the last. One minute, you're standing tall, confident, and ready to take on the world. The next, you're sprawled on the ground, knocked flat on your back, gasping for breath, and frantically groping for some semblance of balance.

But, as the famous saying goes, 'When life gives you lemons, make lemonade.' It's an invitation to seize adversity and turn it into an opportunity to find the silver lining in every cloud. But what if life's lemons are so sour that making lemonade becomes unbearable? What if the lemonade stand you've set up gets knocked down by a gust of wind?

I found myself grappling with these questions not long before what was supposed to be the happiest day of my life: my wedding day. Before that, there was job loss. It wasn't a result of poor performance or company-wide budget cuts. Rather, it sprouted from a moral dilemma, an issue of integrity. My disputes concerning food safety regulations at the restaurant I worked for resulted in a mutual parting of ways. The loss of my job was a gut punch. It was more than just losing a stable income; it shook the foundation of my belief in standing up for what is right.

Fast-forward a week, an ordinary trip to the

grocery store spiraled into a nightmare as I found myself involved in a car accident. This wasn't just a minor scrape; my beloved orange companion of many years was reduced to a wreck. The impact of the accident served as a harsh reminder of the unpredictable turns of fate.

To top it all off, just as my wife and I were basking in the afterglow of our honeymoon, we returned to find our furnace broken. The cozy nest we'd left behind was transformed into an icebox.

Just when life seemed to be settling into an anarchic routine, another calamity presented itself. This time, it was more than just my fortunes on the line; it was my very existence. A motorcycle accident was a dire encounter with mortality that resulted in a traumatic brain injury (TBI). One moment, I was on a regular drive to the gas station, the next, I found myself in a hospital bed, battered and bruised, my memories, thoughts, and emotions in disarray.

The accident occurred eight months into my marriage. This period, which should have been filled with the joy of newlywed bliss and the excitement of building our home, was marred by constant battles against pain, confusion, and fear.

My life seemed to have suddenly plunged into an unending sequence of calamities. It felt as though I was the protagonist in a tragic drama, the universe relentlessly hurling one challenge after another my way. Yet, here's the reality about life's lemons—they don't necessarily become sweeter, but we do grow more proficient at dealing with them.

Life has a way of blindsiding you, of tripping you up when you least expect it. One moment you're upright and steady; the next, you're sprawling on the ground. When you're down, it pounces, landing blow after blow, until it has you in a chokehold. And the strangest part? There's a point at which you stop fighting. You surrender to the hold, let the darkness wash over you, and in a twisted way, it starts to feel... better.

In truth, this is perhaps the most challenging thing I've ever committed to the page. It's not the physical act of typing or forming sentences but the task of laying bare thoughts that are difficult to comprehend, let alone express. I understand them in the solitude of my mind, but translating them into words that convey their true weight and complexity is an entirely different matter.

This isn't a conversation you can casually bring up over a cup of coffee. It's not something you can blurt out amid small talk. It's heavy, it's raw, and it's real. And I've never been this candid about it before. "Hey, I'm contemplating ending it all." There, I've written it. But writing it and saying it, feeling it and living it—those are worlds apart.

This narrative is a conduit, a direct link between my mind and my heart. The thoughts and feelings coursing through this connection are in consensus: we can't do this anymore. The fight, the struggle, the paltry rewards—it's all too much and yet not enough. The question then becomes, why continue? Why keep pushing, keep striving, and keep feigning resilience when all it leads to is this same unbearable point?

I often ask myself: why put my best foot forward and attempt to make this work when I know, deep down, that I can't simply move on? When every step forward feels like trudging through quicksand? This is the crux of my struggle, the heart of my darkness. And it's a darkness that, for better or worse, I'm finally ready to confront.

We each face our litany of challenges in life. They arrive in many forms: the loss of a loved one, the dissolution of a relationship, the stress of financial instability, the sting of betrayal, or the burden of physical or mental illness. These trials are universal in their occurrence yet unique in their impact. They shape us, mold us, and sometimes break us, but they undeniably form the core of our human experience.

When these challenges pile up, when they form a mountain too high to climb, we might find ourselves standing at the precipice of despair, teetering on the edge of our own endurance. It's at this point that we face a choice: to continue the grueling ascent or to let go and succumb to the darkness below.

There's a certain allure to the darkness, an insidious seduction. It promises an end to the pain, the struggle, the never-ending cycle of hope and disappointment. When we're battered and bruised, when every breath feels like a battle, the darkness whispers sweet nothings of release and respite.

So, what happens when we stop fighting? When we let the darkness wash over us and pull us under? It's a surrender of sorts, a relinquishing of control, a quiet acquiescence to the tumultuous sea of despair.

It's also a journey of self-discovery, a voyage into the uncharted territories of our psyche. It's where we confront our deepest fears, our darkest thoughts, and our most desperate desires. But in this confrontation, we also uncover the strength we didn't know we had, the resilience we didn't know we could muster, and the will to survive that defies even our understanding.

But remember, this journey isn't a recommendation but rather a reflection, a contemplation on the profound depths of human suffering and the extraordinary lengths we go to endure, survive, and, perhaps, eventually thrive. As we delve deeper into this discussion, let's bear in mind the weight of these words and the experiences they represent. For they're not just mine—they're ours. We are, after all, all in this together.

As a chef, my life has been a dance with flavors, a symphony of textures, and a canvas of vibrant colors. Post-accident, my universe has contracted, my expansive kitchen replaced by sterile hospital rooms, the medley of kitchen sounds drowned out by medical terminology, and the relentless whisper of my new, unwelcome companion: TBI.

Struggling with the aftermath of the accident involves more than physical healing; it's a daily confrontation with a barrage of side effects that persist in the mundane reality of day-to-day life. Each symptom is an echo of that fateful day, a constant reminder of how much has changed, and a testament to the unseen battles I wage.

I remember a conversation with one of my doctors in the early days of recovery. I was desperate for answers, for some semblance of certainty.

"Doctor," I asked, my voice wobbling with anxiety, "When will I feel like my old self again?"

The answer I received was a harsh initiation into my new reality.

"We don't know," he confessed, his gaze steady but filled with regret. "You may wake up tomorrow and feel fine, or these symptoms could persist indefinitely."

Those words shook me, the uncertainty amplifying my anxiety tenfold. I was adrift in a sea of questions, with no compass to guide me back to the shores of normalcy. The ambiguity of 'we don't know' echoed in my mind, a chilling chorus that underscored my daily battles.

Each day became a gamble. Would I wake up feeling closer to the man I was before the accident, or would I find myself mired deeper in this new, challenging reality? The unpredictability of my symptoms was disorienting. One day, I might find the energy to sit up, to converse, to laugh. The next, the simplest task could be as insurmountable as scaling a mountain.

The journey forward, a path I'm expected to tread, is fraught with challenges. Each step, each effort to progress, feels like moving through quicksand, with the past pulling me back as I strive to inch forward. The vibrant culinary world from before the accident feels like a disconnected dream, replaced by the monochromatic reality of my present.

The weight of my solitude was as sharp as a butcher's knife. Isolation had become my companion during this time, a deliberate choice I'd made. In the aftermath of the accident, there were offers of help and outstretched hands that I could have grasped, but I turned them all away. A misplaced sense of martyrdom had made me reject their goodwill; I didn't want to become a burden, an object of pity. The divorce had severed the one tie I'd relied on, leaving me feeling more alone than ever. The uncertainty of ever stepping back into a kitchen, the fear of never regaining the old normalcy, was deafening in its silence. The future looked like a shadowy abyss, and the thought of suicide, a monstrous concept once, now began to creep insidiously into the recesses of my mind. It was in this bleak solitude that the enormity of my despair truly unfolded.

But it's the night that unveils the rawest parts of this journey. Alone with my thoughts, the world asleep, the darkness outside mirrors the turmoil within. The quiet intensifies the internal chaos, the silence punctuated by the dissonant thoughts that stem from my condition. And on the worst of these nights, my hand strays toward the loaded gun by my bedside.

This admission isn't a plea for help or a call for sympathy. Rather, it's an unfiltered portrayal of the depths of despair that can accompany a condition like TBI. It's a testament to the endurance of the human spirit, a spirit that persists even when every fiber of my being screams for an end.

The specter of suicide looms large in the silent corridors of my mind. Its shadowy presence is a constant companion, a grim reminder of the depths to which the human psyche can plunge when faced with seemingly insurmountable adversity. I confess that I have, more times than I care to admit, considered surrendering to that beckoning darkness.

These are not easy words to write, and they may be even harder to read. But they are my truth—the raw, unvarnished reality of living with a TBI. I'm sharing this not as a call for help or a plea for sympathy but as a stark illustration of the mental and emotional toll this condition can exact.

In my darkest moments, when the pain is unbearable and the world feels unbearably heavy, I have found solace in an unexpected place. My lifeline, my saving grace, has come in the form of a feline companion. My cat, with her soft purring and warm presence, has been a beacon of hope amidst the storm of my despair.

One night, I remember, the darkness was particularly dense, the pain especially sharp. I was at the edge, teetering on the precipice of oblivion. But just as I was about to succumb, my cat jumped onto my lap.

My cat, who had always shown a distinctive preference for my ex-wife's company, seemed to break character.

Her soft, comforting weight grounded me—a lifeline was thrown out to a man drowning in a sea of despair.

As she settled down, purring gently, her simple presence cut through the darkness. Her warm body against mine, her trusting eyes looking up at me, reminded me of something I had nearly forgotten: connection. She reminded me that despite the pain, despite the despair, I was not alone.

A cat curling up on a lap may seem inconsequential, but to me, it was everything. It was a reminder of life and love. It was a moment that pulled me back from the edge—a moment that saved my life.

Chapter 10

Better Days Ahead

"Yesterday is not ours to recover, but tomorrow is ours to win or lose."

- Lyndon B. Johnson

"Onto better days." This phrase has grown into a life motto for me. It's a mantra, a beacon guiding me through the foggy moments, offering me solace. I've learned to hang on to the hope that tomorrow will be a better day, and it's that hope that fuels my every waking moment.

Each day, I weave this mantra into my thoughts because I truly believe it's this optimism that propels me forward. The conviction that today is a good day and tomorrow will be even better is the essence of my motivation. It's a small drop of inspiration that ripples through the vast ocean of my life, instigating waves of positivity and enthusiasm.

This motivation is potent—potent enough to dictate my routine. I find myself saying, "Yes, I'm motivated. I'm off to the gym," or "I'm going to have a fantastic meal today," or "I'm going to catch up with friends." It triggers a domino effect in my life, one positive action leading to another, creating a harmonious symphony of fulfilling moments.

I've noticed that even with this great reservoir of motivation, it's easy to get swept away, to lose sight of the shore. This drive, as beneficial as it is, can sometimes become blinding, like an overbearing spotlight that obscures the surroundings. I've often found myself so engrossed in a project, so intent on completion, that I lose sight of other commitments. On these days, I might forget a planned outing with a friend or neglect my scheduled dog walk.

Yet, I often question, is this such a bad thing? Is it terrible to be so consumed by motivation that you momentarily lose track of your schedule? Isn't it acceptable for minor things to slip when you're fueled by such immense energy and drive?

In this era, I've found myself juggling many balls—work, management, and personal life. My plate is full to the brim, and yet, it's a welcome contrast from the stark predictions of my past. I recall the doctors' gloomy forecasts: "You'll have to get used to doing nothing." Today, however, I'm a whirlwind of action, maintaining a balance of four to five jobs.

I find myself, on any given day, darting from Cleveland to Canton, then Akron, and sometimes back to Canton. The day stretches long into the night, filled with work both outside and at home. Yet, through it all, I maintain a buoyant spirit, a smile that refuses to dim. Each day concludes with a silent affirmation: "It was a good day. Tomorrow will be better."

The mantra persists, embedding itself in my thoughts, my words, and even my social media posts. "Onto better days," I often write, as if the phrase is not just a declaration but a prophecy. I believe we're all journeying toward our better days, each in our own unique way.

The real challenge, however, lies in sustaining

that motivation, that energy, that drive that assures you of a better tomorrow. There are no guarantees in life; tomorrow may or may not be better. It's a realization that harks back to the very first chapter of this book, where we explored the notion of time as an irrelevant concept.

Navigating through life, we all encounter those dark days. Despite everything going well, shadows can creep in, casting doubt on the promise of a better tomorrow. It's a struggle to maintain that hopeful voice in the back of your head, incessantly whispering, "Onto better days."

What does 'better' even mean? If today is a day of rest, of doing nothing, allowing your body and mind to rejuvenate, does that make tomorrow a better day? Can a day of recovery set the stage for a more fruitful tomorrow? Can the act of resetting your mind and recharging your body pave the way for a day that is better by virtue of being more productive, and more filled with action?

But what happens when tomorrow turns out to

be a bad day? How do we reset our minds, brush off the dirt, and say, "No matter how bad today was, tomorrow will be better?"

It's a mindset that demands resilience. When the proverbial shit hits the fan, it takes a certain strength to affirm that tomorrow will be better. I believe those who can maintain this outlook, despite the odds, have uncovered a kernel of true happiness. They've harnessed the power of motivation, the drive that whispers, "Work this out. Make it happen."

To sustain this motivation, perhaps we need to map out life in a way that allows us to understand why things happen. Perhaps we need to experience certain moments, dark days included, to arrive at this outlook. It's from my dark days, times when I flirted with the idea of ending my own life, that I've learned to appreciate the better days. I can look back at those moments and say with conviction that today is a better day, an okay day.

Yet, it's crucial to note that not everyone needs to reach the brink of despair to learn the value of better days. No one should have to contemplate suicide to attain this mindset—that's no way to live. So, the struggle remains: how to instill this motivation, this optimism, without needing to scrape rock bottom?

I'm still grappling with this question, still learning to anchor this mindset so firmly that I can say with unshakeable certainty: I'm onto better days.

It's a curious concept to maintain because when we're happy, we radiate a warmth that others can bask in. When we're motivated, energetic, and having a good time, our positivity is contagious. It brushes off on those around us, uplifting them too.

Perhaps surrounding myself with people who wake up each morning, look at the day ahead and say, "It's going to be a good day," is the answer. If I keep their optimistic energy within my circle, maybe I'll be more inclined to believe that I, too, will have a good day.

It's a challenging theory to validate, but I'm committed to giving it a shot. Each day, I'll strive to affirm that tomorrow will be better. Even if today was a bad day, that's okay. Bad days happen. The real test lies in how we respond to these bad days, and how we spin the negativity into something positive. Maybe that's the birthplace of 'better days.'

Perhaps the true essence of life is found in this transformation—taking the bad moments, extracting the lessons they hold, and using them to make the future brighter. From there on, life becomes a canvas of sunshine and rainbows, a realm of ceaseless joy.

Maybe my motivation was always within me, lying dormant, waiting for the right moment to emerge. Maybe it took all this time, all these experiences, for me to truly learn how to live, how to embrace life in all its complexity. If that's what it took, then so be it. Every moment of struggle was worth it for the clarity it brought.

Now, I'll strive to make every second count, to live life to the fullest, harnessing every ounce of my capacity.

Chapter 11

I'm Terrified of Wasting Your Time

"The greatest mistake you can make in life is to continually fear that you will make one."

- Elbert Hubbard

The chapter unfurls like a revelation, the way morning light seeps into a dark room, illuminating corners once shrouded in obscurity. It's titled 'I'm Terrified of Wasting Your Time'—an admission, a confession, a plea.

It is at this juncture in my journey, as words tumble onto pages and paragraphs take form, that I find the courage to delve into the labyrinth of my past relationships, my marital journey, and my present relationship status. I draw back the curtain, allowing the world a glimpse into the fragility of my emotions, a window into my soul I've guarded zealously.

We are no strangers to this profound feeling, are we? It's almost universal—a language spoken by everyone but acknowledged by very few. It's a lingering shadow in our lives, creeping into our conversations and tinting our interactions with hues of self-doubt. The persistent worry, like a stone in a shoe, that we may be squandering someone's time.

The feeling isn't confined within the borders of romantic relationships; it's a specter that haunts every corner of our lives—the personal, the professional, and every arena where we exchange time, energy, and emotion with others. It's a dance we've all partaken in at least once, this delicate waltz of worthiness, punctuated by the steady beat of an ever-ticking clock.

Now, it's easy to argue that the sensation is a two-way street. We're equally likely to entertain thoughts of others wasting our time, but I wish to steer clear of that notion for this discourse. I want to cast a spotlight on the terror we harbor within us, that we are the ones robbing others of their precious time.

Life's cyclical nature sees us repeat this pattern time and again. 'Am I worthy?' This question, so simple yet loaded, looms ominously over us. The demon of inadequacy slumbers in the pit of our stomachs, rousing to life with every whisper of failure, every murmur of falling short of expectations.

In the face of such thoughts, the terror is palpable. The heart recoils, like a delicate bloom touched by frost, at the very idea of being an obstacle in someone else's journey. Yet, once this seed of self-doubt takes root, it grows, spreading its tendrils around our thoughts until we are haunted by the fear of wasting not just their time but ours too. The realization dawns, as unnerving as a crack of thunder in a silent night—the dread isn't merely of wasting time; it's the terror of wasting life.

The specter of those early chapters, where I wrestled with the demons of depression and dissociation, echo ominously in the backdrop of these reflections. When thoughts like these—insidious whispers telling you that you aren't worth it—begin their relentless assault, they drive you into a cavernous void, stripping away your sense of self.

I found myself tumbling down this very abyss, a free fall into the bleak pit of self-deprecation and apathy. I'd look at my reflection and see an apparition, someone who was draining the life out of others, a phantom tethered to their reality. I'd sit, or rather lie, in the echo chamber of my negativity, my existence reduced to an endless cycle of medications and sleep.

Buried under blankets, I was the ghost haunting my own life, a prisoner of my own body and mind, and my days were swallowed up in the abyss of disassociation. The hours stretched out, endless and uneventful, yet heavy with the weight of my tormented thoughts. My existence seemed insignificant, a mere blip on the radar of life. Who would bother to reach out to me? Why would anyone invest their time and energy in me?

The shadows of these debilitating thoughts began to cast their long, grim shade on my marriage, turning a bond once filled with love into a battleground of unspoken insecurities. I felt like an anchor, a weight that was anchoring my ex-wife to the seafloor of unfulfilled dreams and stagnation.

I found myself retreating further into my shell, my actions (or lack thereof) mirroring my internal struggle. The six to eight hours when I was conscious were punctuated by feelings of helplessness and frustration, and each waking moment was steeped in the bitterness of my self-imposed isolation. On a good day, consciousness would stretch to eight hours, a day where the world wasn't entirely swallowed by darkness.

But even then, I was stagnant and inert. I saw myself as a boulder, lodged stubbornly on a steep hill, making no progress, offering no momentum. Just there, occupying space, going nowhere. The chilling realization was more than unsettling; it was paralyzing, transforming my existence into a series of empty moments ticking by on the clock of life.

In the hushed theater of my mind, I saw myself not as a character enacting the play of life but rather as a moss-covered rock — untouched, immovable and disregarded. I was inert, nestled on the riverbed of existence, the river of life roaring above me, its frothy currents swirling and surging in a ceaseless dance of change and progress. Yet I remained obstinate and unchanging, the moss of my failures and inadequacies growing thicker and denser with each passing day.

This realization didn't dawn gently; it didn't break softly like a summer morning. No, it struck with the cold brutality of a winter gale, icy fingers penetrating my very marrow. It was a gut-wrenching jolt that turned my internal world into a frozen wasteland, encasing my fledgling hope and wilting self-belief in thick ice. It cemented in me the belief that I was less of a participant and more of an obstacle in others' journeys — a hindrance, a stumbling block, a detour around which they must navigate to continue their path.

When my doctors echoed my fears, offering no concrete hope of recovery, the dread deepened into an insidious undercurrent that undermined my faith in my worthiness. As they murmured about the uncertain future and the likelihood of never returning to work, the final nails were driven into the coffin of my self-esteem. Who would want someone who couldn't work? Who would choose to be with someone confined to a bed, a husk of the person they once fell in love with?

Thus, the narrative of my life continued its tortuous journey, culminating in the inevitable dissolution of my marriage. Even as the legalities of divorce were settled, the echo of my insecurities reverberated in the cavernous emptiness of my heart. It's been over two years since then, and yet the scars of my past failures remain, their imprint still fresh in my mind.

Even now, the gears of my thoughts grind against the corrosive fear of being unworthy. The possibility of dating again triggers a cascade of self-doubt. Even as my life continues its frantic pace, juggling five jobs at a time, the question remains: Am I worth someone's time?

The veneer of my constant activity might seem

appealing, indicative of a life brimming with energy and ambition. But the reality is different. The reality is a crushing sense of inadequacy that haunts even the most mundane parts of my life. When I'm home with my pets and my little family, I feel like I'm failing them, too, robbing them of the attention and care they deserve. Maybe six hours of companionship in a day seems generous, but in my heart, it falls short of what they deserve.

So here I sit, wrestling with these gnawing uncertainties, feeling like I can't even meet the silent, unconditional expectations of my pets. If I find myself wanting in their non-judging eyes, how can I hope to fulfill the complexities of another human's needs and desires?

Should I invite a woman into the whirlwind of my life? Lure her with the promise of a date that might be engaging, entertaining, or even warm, only to warn her that the next could be six weeks away. I am perpetually caught in the vice-like grip of my demanding schedule, a captive of my ceaseless pursuit.

The persistent headache, the companion of my 24/7 existence, punctuates each of my waking hours. The intermittent bouts of insomnia, an unwelcome visitor that overstays. I contemplate these tormentors and think, "Why should I impose this burden on someone else?"

Why should I pull someone else into the vortex of my struggles and have her bear witness to the disarray of my life as I grapple to find some semblance of control? It is this poignant introspection that compounds my belief that I am undeserving and that I cannot share my life when I am still fumbling to understand it myself.

It's true; everyone carries their baggage, each case a unique tapestry of personal trials and tribulations. I've heard it said by therapists and well-meaning friends alike. Yet, how can I expect someone else to help shoulder my burdens when they threaten to topple me?

I am still wrestling with the aftermath of the accident, the painful memories that come unbidden, the crushing migraines, and the residual anger simmering beneath the surface. Until I can confidently say, "Yes, I've got this," I will remain entrapped in this self-deprecating cycle. Stuck in this constant refrain: I'm not worth it. I'm going to waste your time.

Until I can wrestle my way out of these intangible chains of self-doubt that wind their cold steel around my thoughts, until I can stand before my reflection and see something more than a potential burden staring back at me, I remain rooted in this quagmire of uncertainty. It is as if I've been encased in ice, frozen in a moment of time, my life's narrative on pause, caught in the grip of my insecurities.

So, there it is—my life, stripped bare and exposed under the harsh glare of reality. It's as if the veneer of pretense has been painfully peeled away, leaving behind the raw, unvarnished truth. This moment, like a stark monochrome photograph in a vibrantly colored album, is jarring and uncomfortable. Yet, it feels like the right place to insert a bookmark, to pause and reflect on the journey so far.

Perhaps, as you peer into this honest snapshot of my life, you might catch glimpses of your struggles reflected in its depths, like echoes bouncing back from a canyon wall. Maybe you'd see the familiar contours of self-doubt, the shadows of lingering fears, or the faint traces of past battles fought and lost. Maybe then, my vulnerability would not just be a solitary echo but a shared symphony resonating with your own life's music.

Chapter 12

Pre TBI

*"Cooking is at once child's play and adult joy.
And cooking done with care is an act of love."*
– Craig Claiborne

Often, I find myself on the receiving end of an almost predictable question, "Why do you cook?" It echoes through every corner of my life, brimming with genuine curiosity and confusion. People can't quite grasp the why behind my profession. They've seen the stereotypical portrayal of kitchen life on TV: it's grueling, it's relentless, it's practically a combat zone.

Yes, the life of a cook is characterized by long, unforgiving hours that span early mornings to late nights. Holidays are a far-fetched dream. It's a toil in a hot, dangerous environment where burns and cuts are almost rites of passage. The constant yelling when someone's food order is amiss becomes a harsh symphony we play on repeat. Stress emanates from every corner: the customers, the owners, the bosses, and even the other staff.

Drama isn't confined to these four walls. The food suppliers have their share of it. Unpaid bills, missing items on the truck, or simply a screw-up by a sales representative—all contribute to the growing mound of stress. Variables beyond control introduce a level of unpredictability that perpetually keeps the kitchen on its toes.

So why do it? What could possibly justify diving headfirst into this vortex of chaos?

For me, the answer lies in how I perceive food. It isn't merely a consumable to satiate hunger, to fill a belly because it growls. To me, food is much more.

For me, sitting down to a good meal transcends the ordinary; it's an extraordinary stress reliever that often gets overlooked. It takes me back to my childhood, back to the hallowed Saturdays at my great-grandmother's house—a sanctuary of joy, love, and delicious food. Those were the happiest times for my family.

My great-grandma was the heart of these beautiful moments. She was kind, funny, and an extraordinary cook. Her recipes were an expression of her love for us. The zucchini bread she made from scratch, and the occasional lamb for my mother, who adored it, are the memories that have shaped me.

I noticed, even as a young child, that these meals were the glue that held us together. Around that table, with a plate of home-cooked food in front of us, we were the happiest. The stress of the outside world melted away; the only thing that mattered was the plate in front of us and the family around us.

This, this right here, is why I cook. I cook to recreate those precious moments. To make a pause in the hustle of life and reduce the stress, if only for a little while. I cook to bring people together, to create a moment when a plate of delicious food takes center stage, and suddenly, all seems well with the world.

The allure of a good meal is undeniable, a respite that makes you forget the woes of an impending workday or a canceled vacation. When a meal is so good that you yearn for another plate, that's when you understand my reason for cooking. I dream of a world where food plays such a significant role, where it isn't just a causal necessity for nutrition but a medium for much more.

Food has an exceptional quality—it can relieve the stress of the outside world and, at the same time, act as a key that unlocks long-forgotten memories. It's a sensory experience that transports you back in time, back to moments that had slipped through the cracks of memory.

Let's simplify it. You sit down for a humble dish of mac and cheese. It isn't just any mac and cheese; this one is special. It brims with layers of rich cheese, perfectly cooked noodles, and a finish of light, creamy butter. This dish doesn't just satisfy your hunger—it catapults you back to a time of innocence.

You're transported back to those youthful Sunday mornings, ensconced on the couch. The mac and cheese isn't just a dish—it's a time machine, it's comfort, it's a slice of nostalgia. A good lamb takes me back to those days with my great-grandma. A simple but soulful meal unfurls the memories of those joyous Saturday nights with my family. Food holds an unparalleled power to achieve this level of connection, and it's this power that inspires me to cook. It brings to life those little moments that felt so ordinary then but feel extraordinarily special now. That's the magic of food.

Now, I wish I could say that my culinary journey began with a grand title like Executive Chef, but we all know that's not how it works. Every job demands you to start from scratch, build your foundation, and gradually climb up. So that's what I did—I started from the ground.

One of my first jobs was at Subway. Yes, you heard it right—Subway. As a 'Sandwich Artist,' as they call it, I had my first taste of the culinary world. And surprisingly, I didn't hate it. There were moments when I found joy in creating my meals, experimenting with different toppings, and giving wings to my creativity.

The next chapter in my culinary journey took

me to Shady Hollow Country Club. I joined as a line cook, juggling between my job and high school. I was also a part of the culinary arts course at RG Drage Career Technical Institute, which helped me experience the best of both worlds. I was still figuring out what I wanted from life, and cooking began to shape up as a promising prospect.

Juggling high school culinary classes with my job at the country club, I was soaking up every bit of industry knowledge. The heat, the chaos, the adrenaline—it was all incredibly addictive. The beating of my heart in sync with the frenzied tempo of a Friday night service in a sweltering 110-degree kitchen, sauté pans flying, flames leaping as alcohol met hot pans—these were the moments that fed my passion.

I wanted more, craved more. This led me to the Culinary Institute of America in Hyde Park, New York—arguably the best in the world for culinary arts. The motto there, "food is life," resonated with me deeply. Every step on that campus was a step towards food; every class was an exploration of this culinary universe.

One of the classes that stayed with me was Product Knowledge. There, we studied food, its anatomy, and its intricacies. I remember passing around different food items, studying them, and understanding their nature. We delved into mushrooms, their porous nature, and their chemical structure. We didn't just stop there; we studied fruits, herbs, and everything down to the minutest detail.

Another class had us playing butchers. We broke down cows from start to finish. We did the same with fish and just about any other animal you can think of. Each class was a new journey into the depth of food and its wonders. Each class fueled my love for cooking, my love for food, and the magic it carries.

We studied everything that was food-related, be it ingredients, cooking techniques, or the art of pairing food and wine. Every day felt like an exhilarating step up from the last. One day, I was mastering the five mother sauces—Béchamel, Espagnole, Hollandaise, Tomato, and Velouté—and the next day, I was learning their countless derivative sauces. The following days were spent figuring out how to pair those sauces with chicken and, subsequently, which wines went best with them.

This was more than just an education; it was the foundation of my future in food, and I relished every moment of it. We were located just an hour's train ride outside of New York City, which opened up a whole new world of culinary exploration. My friends and I would journey into the city, exploring its diverse food landscape. We'd hop from one restaurant to the next, savoring street food and indulging in the city's gastronomic diversity.

On weekends, we'd take a different route. We'd stroll up to a nearby farmer's market, randomly pick up fresh produce, and challenge ourselves to create something extraordinary. Our passion for food was immense. It was like an insatiable entity within us that continuously craved growth, an unstoppable force eager to expand its boundaries. It was an aspiration, a driving force that defined our love for food.

But that was our love for food. We yearned for it to grow continuously, and so we pursued every opportunity that could stretch our boundaries, ignite our creativity, and enrich our knowledge. It was truly an incredible experience.

After completing my first year, a small hiccup arose. Originally, I had planned to delve into it here, but I've decided against it. I want to keep the spirit of this chapter uplifted, so I'll save that story for another time.

Post my first year. I was fortunate to secure an internship at Fenway Park in Boston. I was positioned in their high-tier culinary program, catering to guests in the suite rooms and other premium spaces. It was an engaging and enriching experience that exposed me to an entirely new facet of the culinary world. We got creative, from roasting whole pigs to experimenting with a variety of fish, which charged my passion for food even further.

I had always been a country boy and had always said I would never live in a city. Yet, there I was, thriving in Boston, Massachusetts, walking to work, catching trains, and immersed in city life. And much to my surprise, I loved it. The energy of a city like Boston was contagious. In my opinion, it's one of the best cities I've ever been to. The vibrancy, the fervor, and the love within that city were simply extraordinary.

However, I had to confront an unfortunate reality after concluding my internship. Due to some medical issues, I had to step away from culinary school. It was a decision I didn't make lightly, but it was a necessary one.

Despite the unexpected turn of events, I was undeterred. I was determined to acquire the knowledge and skills I would have gained with the degree without actually possessing it. I was driven to keep learning and to never stop. That's a mindset I still hold dear today. Eight years later, I am as committed as ever to self-improvement and lifelong learning.

When I returned home following my medical leave, I found myself drawn back to Shady Hollow. I took on a role as a kitchen manager, a position that gave me my first taste of leadership in the culinary industry.

Not long after, the executive chef, who I'd come to consider a good friend, decided to move on to other opportunities.

Recalling my pledge to challenge myself constantly, I decided to seize the moment. I walked into the general manager's office and announced my desire for the executive chef position. Looking back, it was an incredibly audacious move, perhaps one of the most overconfident declarations I've ever made. In truth, I was nowhere near prepared for such a demanding role. I was 20 years old, a mere novice in culinary years, boldly declaring my intention to take on the formidable responsibility of being an executive chef.

He should have told me to shut the fuck up and get out of his office. Those should have been his words. But instead, he gave me a shot. He gave me an opportunity, something that I truly wasn't expecting. And I can't even tell you how fucking honored I was to even have the brief second of him saying, "Sure, why not?"

And you know what? I busted my ass to learn

that position. I was working almost 18 hours a day learning. I was hitting the books, figuring out everything from management, recipe costing, true menu costing, wine pairings, and everything I could. How to properly manage and schedule staff, all of it.

And somehow, I managed to pull it off. At 20 years old, I pulled off being an executive chef. I was way too young. I had interviews with potential hires, older, more experienced chefs who walked out of interviews because they said, "I'm not working for a kid." Or those who said they didn't want to work with me because they were sure I had no fucking clue what I was doing.

I even had people tell me I was stupid for taking that job because they believed I was probably going to ruin the club. But, turns out, the next three years at Shady Hollow Country Club were some of the best years they'd had in two decades.

Now was that a hundred percent because of me? Hell no, but I'd like to think I threw my hat in the ring and was a part of that.

So, here I am today, still an executive chef, standing strong at the ripe age of 28. I've started my own spice company, and I am on the brink of opening my barbecue restaurant. I'm even preparing to launch a series of cooking classes.

But as I stand on the threshold of these new ventures, I must take a moment to express my deep gratitude. I've put countless hours, sweat, tears, and passion into getting to where I am today. However, my journey is not a solitary one. People in my life have taken larger risks on me than they should have. I'm blessed because without those people, without their faith, without them seeing something in me that perhaps I couldn't see at the time, I might not be where I am today.

Had they not taken those risks, I might have walked away from cooking. I might have sought another degree, ventured into a different profession, or tried something different. But they gave me a shot. And not only did I take it, but I grabbed it with both hands and ran with it with everything I had.

I am truly, deeply honored and humbled by my journey thus far. The culinary world is not a forgiving one; it's fast, it's hot, it's relentless. But it's also one filled with immense creativity, limitless potential for growth, and a profound sense of achievement that I wouldn't trade for anything else.

The last eight years have been an absolute whirlwind of growth, learning, and self-discovery. They have shaped me, challenged me, and at times, pushed me to the very edge. But they've also been the most rewarding, fulfilling, and exciting years of my life.

As I look forward to the future, I can't help but feel a buzz of anticipation. If the last eight years have been anything to go by, then the next eight years promise to be a thrilling journey filled with more learning, more cooking, and more exploring the fantastic world of food.

So, bring it on. I'm ready, armed with my chef's knife and a burning passion for food, ready to take on the culinary world and make my mark. Here's to the next eight years!

Chapter 13

A Letter to Life

Dear Life,

I am writing this letter to inform you that I have mixed emotions. I am torn on the message you are trying to send me. Sometimes, I'm not sure if you are trying to help me or set me back. I feel as if you want to keep me moving, but I don't know if it's forward or backward.

Here I am, writing to you as if you were a close friend. Someone who I haven't talked to in years but a friend I would love to catch up with.

Truthfully, I feel like you are an unreliable narrator in this life.

Things are generally complicated with you. It's like you enjoy watching me have a hard time. You have this way of trickling in little glimpses of happiness—moments where I feel like you are attempting to see me have some kind of peace.

Then you sweep the leg. The fallacious feeling of things being correct. That little bit of happiness, you take it from me, and you hide it so I cannot find it.

This cycle, this sequence of emotions that do not have a proper home, eats away at me.

I want to continue being your friend. I would like to say that we could even be family. I truly believe that we can get along; maybe we just need some work.

Because internally, I do think you want to help me. I'm just confused about your training methods. This isn't a new Rocky movie. I can usually take the punches you throw; I think I just need some more training rounds.

Then again, maybe that's what you are doing—training me. Even though it feels like you enjoy watching me hurt, maybe you are trying to make me stronger overall. Because you and I go rounds.

Sometimes I win. I start the next round with the vitality of having won the match.

We go back and forth. In reality, I wasn't supposed to make it this long. You had me marked as a dead man at 25. Yet, here I am, pushing forward, continuing on this road in life without a map, trying my hardest to determine which left or right turn I should make.

Maybe I actually have to thank you for that. The fact that I'm lacking direction, or I feel as if I'm lacking direction. When in truth, I think you put me through these hard situations to show me where I can go. I'm at this stage in my life where I'm doing everything I can to live to the fullest. I act as if I'm not going to make it home tonight. I act as if today may be my last day.

That, I do thank you for. With that mindset, it has helped push me into a whole new world of possibilities. You've got me maximizing the amount of time I have. Maybe it's one day, maybe it's 50 years. Either way, I'm going to make the most of it.

I guess what I'm trying to say here is, even though you confuse me, thank you. I've concluded that this is just part of dealing with you. We take the good and the bad, the highs and the lows, and we persevere. Those rounds where we think you won are you just prepping us for the next fight.

In retrospect, this dead man walking thanks you. I know sometimes I yell at you, and sometimes I try to fight back. But I think from now on, I'll just accept what you give me and make the best outcome.

So, Life, from me to you, you are my friend. I'm happy with all the blessings you've shown me, I'm happy with all the hardships you've given me, and I'm ready for what you have next. Good or bad.

I sign this letter with my overall appreciation. Appreciation for the road you've given me. No matter how rocky, I do not believe I would have done half the things I'm currently doing without those hard times. I now focus on mental health support, caring for others, and the overall growth of the people around me. Thank you for changing me into a better person. A more positive person. Someone who is genuinely happy to have a life.

Your dearest friend,

Michael V Jarzenski